**NATIONAL
GEOGRAPHIC**

Worlds of Opportunity

PIONEER EDITION

By Bonnie Brook

CONTENTS

KAKENYA'S DREAM
A Future of Hope

By Bonnie Brook

Kakenya Ntaiya is a National Geographic Emerging Explorer. She has come home to Kenya to make her dream of opportunity come true.

These women walk along the road that leads to Kakenya's village in Kenya.

An eighth-grade girl had a plan. She lived in the small village of Enoosaen in Kenya. She dreamed of going to high school. Then she wanted to attend college in the United States. In return, she promised to come back and help the people of Enoosaen. She begged her parents and the village elders to let her go. Then she left Enoosaen to follow her dream. This girl, Kakenya Ntaiya, became part of a world-wide movement.

Today, more than 3 percent of the world's population live outside their country of birth.

Millions more have moved within their home borders. Many people move to earn money. Some people are forced to move by damage to the environment or by human conflict. Some people move to find opportunities far from home.

One thing is certain. People are on the move like never before. Who are these people? Where are they going? How will they change society? Most importantly, how will their journey change who they are?

A village elder blesses Kakenya's family in Enoosaen.

This boy herds cows outside his village in Kenya.

Kakenya's Dream

Kakenya Ntaiya came to the United States to build a better future for herself and others. Kakenya was not a **refugee**. She did not *have* to leave home. Kakenya chose to go to college in the United States. Her decision to migrate, or move to another country, was **voluntary**. In fact, she had to convince her parents and the village elders to let her go.

Never Forget Her Home

Kakenya was stubborn. She insisted. Kakenya promised the village elders that she would come back. She would repay her community for everything.

Kakenya vowed to build a school for girls in Enoosaen. She would use her knowledge to give girls the chance to get a good education.

"A girl will never forget her home," the elders said. They believed that Kakenya would return to her village.

Kakenya had earned a **scholarship** from Randolph-Macon Woman's College in the United States. But this money was not enough to pay her way to America. So the entire village collected money. They helped to pay for Kakenya's journey. With their blessings, Kakenya set off for college in the United States.

Life in a New Culture

There was much for Kakenya to learn about life in America. She had to do well in her classes. She also had to learn about plumbing, silverware, superstores, and even snow. Friends wanted to take Kakenya to a movie or a fast-food restaurant for the first time.

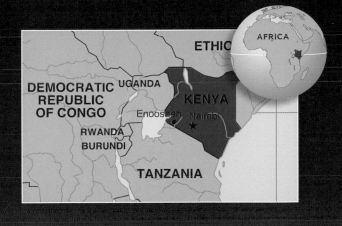

There were other international students at Randolph-Macon Woman's College, too. They had also come to the United States for their education. Kakenya could understand their experiences.

Kakenya knew she had to make the most of her time in the United States. While she was at college, she worked in a computer lab. She also traveled to African Union student conferences. Each day, Kakenya gave thanks to the people at home who had helped her.

Promise to Keep

During this time, Kakenya often felt overwhelmed. The tasks before her were huge. She had to do well in school. She had to repay her village. She had a school for girls to build. When things were tough, Kakenya turned to her friends. She knew they would understand. This always helped Kakenya keep going.

Randolph-Macon Woman's College

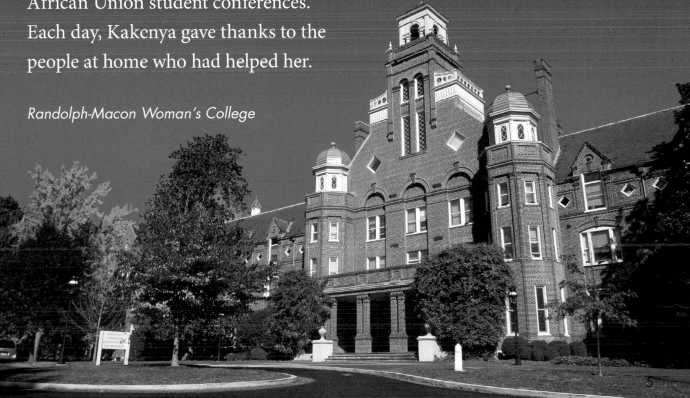

Kakenya reads with girls from her school in Ensoosaen.

Promises Kept

Kakenya completed her studies at Randolph-Macon Woman's College. Next, she decided to study at the University of Pittsburgh. Then she returned home to Enoosaen.

"Today, I am working to fulfill the promise I made years ago. To return to my village and give back," Kakenya says. Since 2006, Kakenya has worked to build a school for girls in Enoosaen. Her school gives young girls the opportunity to get a good education. It also helps them learn to be leaders. "This is my dream," Kakenya says.

Kakenya's school for girls is called the Kakenya Center for Excellence. It opened in May 2009 with 32 students. The school plans to have 150 students in grades four through eight by 2013.

Academics and Leadership

Each grade has its own classroom at the school. The girls learn English and Swahili. They study math, science, geography, and history. They learn about religion and the arts. And they take part in physical education.

The school also offers a leadership program. The girls take part in after-school activities, student councils, and community programs.

Kakenya believes that these experiences will help the girls become more confident.

Preservation of Culture

At the same time, Kakenya's school preserves culture. Girls learn about family and village traditions. They also learn about the latest ways to help their farms, their cows, and their homes. This way, families feel the benefits of the school, too. So a girl's education becomes good for everyone.

What's Next?

Kakenya spends her time working at the school and raising money for it. She enjoys watching her students practice algebra, dance, and sing. They even have fun talking to people over the Internet.

Kakenya believes that her school can help make more dreams come true. She wants the students to go on to high school.

She wants them to receive the same kind of education as students in China, Europe, or America. The parents of Kakenya's students agree. "When I shared that vision with the girls' parents, a round of applause [said] this is a shared dream."

A Long Journey

It's been a long journey for Kakenya. She has made her dream come true. She migrated to the United States. She attended college there. She gained valuable knowledge. Now she has returned home to share this knowledge with others. In the process, Kakenya Ntaiya has reshaped her community and redefined herself.

WORDWISE

refugee: a person who is forced to leave home because it is too dangerous for him or her there

scholarship: money to help you continue studying

voluntary: something that is done because you want to do it, not because you must do it

On the MOVE!

NORTH AMERICA

Vancouver **0.8m**

San Francisco **1.2m**

Los Angeles **4.4m**

Riverside **0.8m**

Houston **1.1m**

Toronto **2.0m**

Chicago **1.6m**

Dallas **1.0m**

Boston **0.7m**

New York 5.1m

Washington **1.1m**

Miami 1.9m

London **1.9m**

Paris **1.0m**

SOUTH AMERICA

Buenos Aires **0.9m**

Number of People Born in Other Countries

- 5 million
- 3 million
- 1.5 million
- 0.8 million

Source: George Washington University–Globalization, Urbanization and Migration (GWU-GUM)

Miami, United States: *Cubans play dominoes in Little Havana. Other newcomers are from Haiti and Jamaica.*

New York, United States: *New York City has the most immigrants anywhere. These new residents make life in New York exciting and diverse.*

IMMIGRATION HAS GONE GLOBAL. People are on the move like never before. Some, like Kakenya Ntaiya, are searching for opportunity. Others are looking for a safe place to live. This map of gateway cities shows where many immigrants go. It also shows that the world has become a truly global community.

St. Petersburg **0.7m**

Moscow **1.6m**

ASIA

EUROPE

Tel Aviv-Yafo **0.7m**

Riyadh **1.5m** Dubai **1.1m**

Jiddah **1.2m**

Hong Kong **3.0m**

AFRICA

Singapore **1.4m**

AUSTRALIA

Sydney **1.2m**

Melbourne **1.0m**

Toronto, Canada: *This shop is in Toronto's Chinatown. Many people come to Toronto from Asian countries like China and India.*

Dubai, United Arab Emirates: *Many workers from India, Pakistan, and Bangladesh find jobs in Dubai. New residents make up a large part of the population there.*

adapted from a report by Brian Reed that aired on NPR's *Morning Edition*, February 16th–17th, 2011

A Sinking Nation Prompts Migration

Natural disasters often strike without warning. People must act. There is little time to think about where to go. A natural disaster is happening right now on the islands of Kiribati. But it is happening slowly. So the islanders can plan what to do.

Kiribati (KEER-uh-buhs) is a country of tiny islands in the Pacific Ocean. The islands are in an area about twice the size of Alaska. South Tawara Island is the nation's capital.

The islands are 2 meters (6.5 feet) above sea level. This makes people worry. Why? Many residents think that temperatures are warmer. They think sea levels are rising. They fear that changes like these will make the islands sink. "The sea level, now it comes to the road, even to the houses," says Ata Merang.

Migrating with Dignity

Kiribati's President Tong is worried about the rising sea levels and other changes. He has a plan to help his citizens. He hopes his plan will give citizens the chance to "migrate with dignity."

President Tong says, "We don't just pack up our people from the villages . . . and say, 'Ok, there you are.' " Instead, he is trying to find a way for people to move slowly.

This young Kiribati resident watches as waves wash into the village.

He wants citizens to adapt to their new surroundings and establish new communities in other countries.

The first step in the plan is called the Kiribati Australia Nursing Initiative (KANI). More than 80 students from Kiribati have gone to study nursing at Australia's Griffith University. Typically, students train and go back home. They then apply their skills to help their country. KANI students might not have a country to go back to.

Living in Another Culture

Tibea Baure is one KANI student. Moving from Kiribati to Australia had its challenges. For one thing, it was too quiet. "Not like back on the island. They shout, and they can sing anytime they want to sing," she says. The silence makes her feel lonely.

Another KANI student found it hard to sleep on a bed. Instead, she slept on the traditional woven mat that she brought from Kiribati. "I have to sleep on the floor!" she announced.

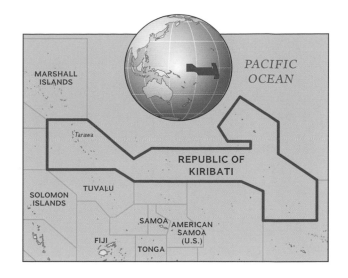

Preserving a National Identity

Many older residents of Kiribati do not think that the islands are sinking. Tibea wants her parents to move to Australia. But they don't think the rising water is a threat. Instead, many Kiribatians are afraid to lose their national identity. What will it mean if their country no longer exists? Who will they be?

KANI students have found one answer. They gather every Wednesday night at someone's home, sit on their mats, and sing island songs. In that way, they remember Kiribati and feel just a little bit closer to home.

Moving On

**People around the globe are on the move.
Answer these questions to join them.**

1 Why did Kakenya want to leave home?

2 What steps did Kakenya take to migrate? List them in order.

3 How is Kakenya helping her community with her knowledge?

4 Why do some people want to leave Kiribati? What is President Tong doing to help?

5 How are Kakenya's and Tibea's stories similar? How are they different?